# *Flora* HEALTH WORKER in ACTION

*by* Charlotte Rolfe and Flora Ngalauka

MACMILLAN

Macmillan Education
Between Towns Road, Oxford OX4 3PP
A division of Macmillan Publishers Limited
Companies and representatives throughout the world

ISBN 0–333–92453–3

Text © Charlotte Rolfe and Flora Ngalauka 2002
Design and illustration © Macmillan Publishers Limited 2002

First published 2002

Illustrations by Maureen and Gordon Gray; Illustrated Arts
Series design by Geoffrey Wadsley; cover by AC Design
Produced for Macmillan Education by Aldridge Press
www.aldridgepress@demon.co.uk

The authors and publishers would like to thank the following for
permission to reproduce their photographs:
Macmillan Malawi pp7, 8 (top) (photographs Govati Nyirenda); Panos,
cover (main picture) and p2 below (photograph Giacomo Pirozzi),
pp16, 19 above and below (photograph Liba Taylor), 21 (photograph
Giacomo Pirozzi); Still Pictures p12 (photograph Heine Pedersen);
Trip Photo Library pp2 (above), 3

Photographs not listed above were provided by the authors.

Printed and bound in Malaysia

2006  2005  2004  2003  2002
10  9  8  7  6  5  4  3  2  1

# Flora says "Welcome!"

Flora's home is just across the valley in this picture. You can see where she lives on the map of Malawi, too. Flora is used to daily life in the rural areas. She walks to work each day, and she helps on the family farm in her spare time.

Flora is a rural health worker. Her office is at the local health centre in Mpemba. She has work to do at the centre, but on most days she also visits villages in the area. Her job is to make sure the people know how to stay well and healthy, and to give advice, information and help where it is needed.

In this book, you can find out more about Flora and her work.

## Malawi

Malawi is one of Africa's smaller countries, but it is much more densely populated than its neighbours, with more than 100 people per square kilometre. More than half its people are less than twenty years old.

Number of people: 10 million
- In towns: 1 million
- In rural areas: 9 million

1

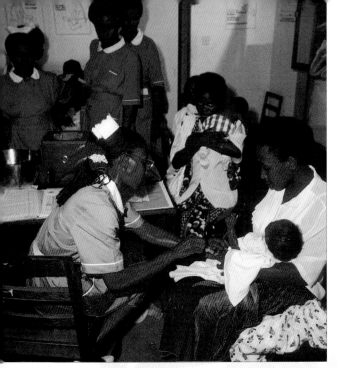

*These babies are having vaccinations to protect them against common diseases.*

Like health workers all over the world, Flora helps local people to prevent and treat the most common health problems in their own homes.

❝Probably the most simple health rule is washing your hands after using the latrine or before touching food – these are things we should learn as children, but we also need to understand *why* this is important. Part of my job is to explain to people how diseases are spread. This gives them the knowledge they need to protect themselves.❞

# *Staying healthy*

When you are sick, you may need to see a doctor or a nurse. But as Flora knows, the most important thing is to stay healthy.

❝I work in primary health care. That means I help people to understand ways of keeping as strong and healthy as possible. This is very important, especially in our rural areas. For many villagers the nearest hospital may be more than a day's journey away, and the cost of medicines is more than most people can pay.❞

*Washing hands outside the latrine.*

Most communities have their own traditional ideas about healthy living. Every health worker needs to be aware of these. Some traditional medicines can be very effective, and Flora is careful to build on the knowledge and skills that the community already has. At the same time, she is ready to explain why some practices may be harmful.

❝Because I work in my home area, people know that I am part of the community, and share their problems and their culture. At the same time, I have to set an example and earn their respect and trust.❞

*A traditional healer at work.*

## Helping the sick

A health worker is often the first person in the community to recognise signs of a dangerous illness. Many of the villages that Flora visits are far from main roads. She is the link between the village and the nearest clinic or hospital.

❝I have to understand what I can and can't do myself, and when to ask for help from the medical staff at the health centre.❞

3

*Flora's primary school at Mpemba now has two new classrooms. Afternoon football is still as popular as ever.*

# Starting out

Flora was the eighth of nine children – so she had many older brothers and sisters. However, each of the children had their own duties at home on the farm.

❝As a small girl, my job was to look after the cows. They were very important to us because we used to sell their milk to the local dairy. That money paid for the household things we needed such as soap, cooking oil and other things we couldn't produce ourselves on the farm.❞

Every schoolday, Flora walked six kilometres to Mpemba Primary School. She carried the cows' milk to the dairy, which was near the school.

❝I liked school, but I was often very tired because I had to get up very early to milk the cows first, before bathing and going to school. There was a lot to do, and I was often late.❞

But Flora's teacher encouraged her. Flora's eldest brother, who was working in Blantyre, helped the family too, by sending money home.

> **❝** Soon we began to depend very much on my brother because one by one our cows died, until there was only one left. Then that one died too – it was my fault, I had given it mangoes to eat, but I hadn't removed the big seeds first, and they caused a blockage in the cow's stomach. Of course, my mother was really worried – how would we manage now? **❞**

Flora's mother was able to earn some money by cutting small stones from the local quarry and selling them for road-building. Flora used to help her. It was hot and dusty work, but it helped to keep the family going.

*Flora could read well by the time she was in Standard 2. As a schoolgirl she often read the Bible at home with her mother.*

## Malaria

Malaria is carried by mosquitoes and causes a very high fever. Mosquitoes lay their eggs in still water. To stop this people can:

- fill up nearby holes or pits with sand.
- cover all water containers.
- bury all empty, unwanted containers where water can collect.

## A trip to hospital

When Flora was eleven years old, she became very ill with malaria and was rushed to hospital.

> **❝** I felt frightened because I was sick, and the people in the ward were strangers to me. But there was one young nurse who was very kind. Before she gave me my injection, she explained carefully what she was going to do and how it would help – even though the injection was going to hurt a bit. I completely trusted her, and hospital was alright after that! **❞**

After two days, Flora was much better and it was time to go home.

> **❝** I said goodbye to the nurse, and told her that I'd like to be a nurse too, when I grew up. She told me to work hard and finish my education. I didn't forget her good advice. **❞**

# A chance to succeed

When Flora was growing up, there were very few secondary schools in her country.

Like many other young Malawians, she was unable to get a place in a government secondary school. But she didn't give up.

❝My mother was willing to help me, and I wanted to do a job that would make a real difference in my community. My aunt, who was a nurse, told me that I must complete Form Four if I wanted to work in health care.❞

*Flora (left) with a classmate at Nankumba.*

So Flora decided to take the one opportunity she had – to go to a distance education centre.

Here she would study from Form One to Form Four – it wouldn't be the same as going to a government secondary school, but she could at least take the national exams at the end of the time.

Flora therefore enrolled as a day student at Nankumba Distance Education Centre which was near her home. She joined a class of 80 students in Form One. There were only six teachers at the centre, and they supervised all the classes between them.

❝We studied the usual subjects – I liked English, maths and biology best. We had to pay for the notes we used, and to take the exams. We also had to pay money to the school fund. That was to buy the furniture and materials we used at the centre.❞

## Factfile

### Education in Malawi

Until the mid 1990s about half of the country's children went to primary school, and only one in fifty attended secondary school.

After 1994, Malawi had a new government, and there were some big changes in education.

Many more children began to go to primary school, and more than 20,000 new teachers were trained.

There were special programmes to encourage girl education in particular.

"One day I was too tired to do my assignment and the teacher sent me away. My mother saw me playing when I should have been in class, and she was very angry. But soon after that, I saw a girl I remembered from my primary school. She had not had any secondary education. She was helping her mother to sell firewood. I realised that I had to study harder and learn. Then I could do something that would make a difference to our lives."

*Making a difference: these young community workers are taking part in a training session at one of Malawi's newer community day secondary schools.*

# Getting started

Just before Flora completed Form Four, she talked to a rural health worker who was visiting her village. Flora was interested in this work. She read everything she could about health, and she talked to her aunt about different jobs in health care. Then she found out how to apply for a job as a trainee health worker.

**❝**I travelled to Blantyre for my interview at the District Health Office. I was a bit nervous – not about going to Blantyre, as I had been there often with my sisters – but I wasn't sure what questions the interviewer was going to ask.**❞**

Flora had to answer questions on:
- Malawi's health services.
- the importance of clean water.

**❝**I don't think the interviewer expected me to know everything about the job – there was certainly a lot more to learn.**❞**

Flora was accepted as a health surveillance assistant – a health worker – and she started with a one-day introduction to the work of the Public Health Department.

**❝**Public health is mainly about preventing disease and improving the health of the people. Medicine is mainly about curing people who are sick. In the rural areas, health workers work hand in hand with the medical staff at the health centre; we report to the District Health Inspector in Blantyre.**❞**

## District health care

At the District Health Office:

A **district health inspector** is in charge of public health for each of Malawi's 24 districts.

At the health centre:

A **health assistant** supervises the work of the health surveillance assistants and provides a link between them and the health inspector.

In the village:

The **health surveillance assistant** (health worker) visits the village, gives out information and advice, and reports back on the health of the people there.

# Training

Flora was sent to the health centre at Mpemba as a new health worker. So that she could do her job with knowledge and confidence, she went on a special eight-week training course.

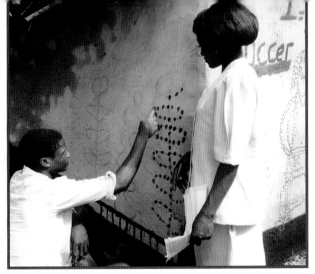

*Taking a pride in the environment. This villager is decorating a newly-built home.*

**"**There were forty new health workers on the course. We had a lot to learn in those weeks. We studied environmental health and hygiene. We also discussed how to mobilise people – how to get them interested in improving their homes and villages. I soon understood that it was important to become a good communicator – a lot of my job was going to be teaching and advising people.**"**

Flora also learnt how to collect and record information for district health records and how to vaccinate people in a safe and hygienic way. She was soon practising those skills in the weekly clinics at the health centre.

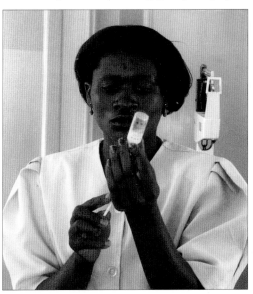

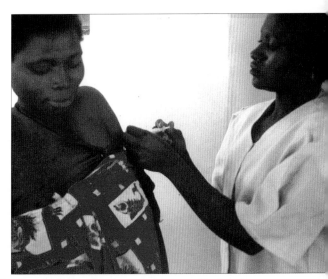

◀ *Flora fills a clean syringe (small plastic tube with needle). After wiping the skin clean, she carefully injects the vaccine.* ▲

# At the health centre...

At the health centre in Mpemba there are eleven health workers. They each visit four to six villages in the area. What other jobs do people do?

*Flora with community nurse, Mrs Mbalame (left) and midwife, Mrs Kampondo (right).*

**The midwife** runs the ante-natal clinic, where pregnant mothers are examined to see if they have any health problems or if the birth might be a difficult one. She helps the mothers during birth, and gives them advice about breastfeeding and caring for their babies. She is an experienced nurse who has completed additional training in delivering babies.

**The community nurse** treats people who come to the clinic with illnesses or injuries. She decides whether patients need to go to a bigger hospital for treatment, or whether they can be treated at the health centre. She organises immunisation programmes, where children come to be vaccinated against common diseases.

**The medical assistant** works in the office of the health centre, and makes sure that the medicines, particularly vaccines, are properly stored and recorded. (Some vaccines have to be stored very cold, in a fridge, or they will not work.) He gives out medicines to patients and assists at clinics.

**Ward attendants** keep the centre clean. The delivery room and the wards must be kept very clean, so that the mothers and their new babies do not get infections.

**Ground workers** keep the compound around the health centre clean and neat. They make sure that all waste from the centre is properly removed, and that no rubbish is left lying around to poison the water supply or attract disease-carrying insects or animals.

10

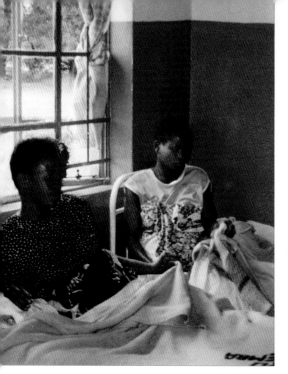

## Healthy mothers, healthy babies

**❝** Every Monday, we have a clinic for pregnant mothers. I always try to encourage women to come to this clinic at least once during their pregnancy. At the clinic we have a chance to check their general health and see if there are any problems. I spend some time talking to them about keeping healthy in pregnancy, and I give them all an anti-tetanus injection which will protect them and their baby. The nurse or midwife carries out medical checks, and we keep a record of the treatment given. **❞**

*These mothers are under medical care in the maternity ward. They will have their babies at the health centre.*

Flora knows that when mothers are pregnant their natural resistance to sickness may be weaker. Some of the women are anaemic and their blood is thin – they need extra iron in their food.

**❝** Iron-rich foods such as meat, fish and eggs are best for a pregnant mother, but these are often too costly for many people. Dark green leafy vegetables are also good, though, and beans, which can be grown at home. We also give mothers special iron tablets in the later stages of pregnancy. **❞**

### Factfile

Tetanus is a very serious disease and can be deadly – even in the world's best hospitals about half the sufferers die. It is caused by a germ that lives in human or animal waste. The germ enters the body usually through a wound – perhaps a bite from an animal or a deep cut caused by treading on something sharp, such as a thorn or a dirty nail.

People can protect themselves against tetanus by having these injections:

- one every month for three months
- one after a year
- one after ten years

# Young children

At the health centre Flora helps to run a weekly one-day clinic for the under-fives.

❝We encourage mothers to bring their babies for weighing, and for their vaccinations. Babies should be vaccinated against the main children's diseases by the time they are one. We record this information on a special health card for each child.❞

*This two-months-old baby is having her first polio vaccine. The risk of polio is highest in the first two years of life.*

## Factfile

### A balanced diet

To be healthy, we need a balanced diet. This means having the right mixture of different kinds of foods.

- We need fresh fruit and vegetables, which contain vitamins for our general health, especially skin, hair and eyesight.

-  We need protein (body-building foods), which we can get from peas, beans, meat, fish and eggs and milk.

- We need carbohydrates (energy-giving foods), such as maize meal and rice.

It is especially important for growing children to have a good, balanced diet, so they form strong bones and are able to resist disease.

When Flora visits villages in her community, she enjoys talking about the crops they are growing. She encourages them to grow peas, beans and green vegetables and add these to the daily maize dish called *nsima*.

Weighing babies regularly is a good way of checking whether they are growing well and getting enough healthy food.

❝Maize meal porridge on its own is not enough – children need fruit and vegetables such as mangoes, sweet potatoes, carrots and papaya, and some protein every day.❞

*Shelling peas from the vegetable garden, ready for a nourishing meal later.*

## Bean soup

This is very good for someone who is recovering from illness, or for small children.

> 1 cup of cooked beans
> 1 tomato
> 1 green onion
> 1 cup of milk (or one small spoon of dried milk and a cup of water)
> salt

Wash and chop the whole onion and the green top as well. Then skin and chop the tomato.
Put the beans, tomato and onion in a pot and cook until all the vegetables are soft. Mash the vegetables with a wooden spoon, and push them through a sieve.
Return the mixture to the pot.
Add the milk and a small amount of salt and stir until the soup begins to thicken.

Flora advises mothers when they come to the clinic and when she visits villages.

❝ Mothers want to give their children the best food possible. Sometimes there may be a problem at home, and children come to us seriously under-nourished. We then keep them at the health centre and feed them with nourishing food until their weight has improved. ❞

*These two children are receiving food at the health centre until they are well enough to return home.*

# A day's work

Flora checks the store of medicines in the fridge at the health centre. Some of these will be used to treat patients in today's TB clinic. Flora helps at the clinic. She reminds patients to attend the clinic regularly. Their treatment may last up to one year.

## Did you know?

TB (short for 'tuberculosis') is a disease which affects people's lungs. Early signs include a bad cough and sweating at night. The sufferer loses weight and becomes very tired.

The disease is very **contagious**. That means it can spread very easily from one person to another. A sufferer must be kept apart from the rest of the household.

TB can kill if it is not treated quickly. Babies and young children should be vaccinated against the disease. People who are weak or undernourished are more likely to get TB.

Flora now sets off for a village visit. She is responsible for six villages and she tries to visit them all once a month. She walks to each one.

When she gets to the village, Flora talks first to the village headman, to announce her visit.

❝In all the villages I seek out people who can form a small group or committee, to take a particular interest in the public health of the village and set a good example to others. Women are very important for the committee because they have a big influence on family health.❞

Through this group, Flora finds out how the village has been getting on since her last visit. She talks to people about their individual health problems, too. She has brought medicine with her for a child who is sick with measles, and she checks up on a TB patient and his family.

Today Flora is also collecting data, or information. With a member of the village health committee, she visits homes in the village. You can see the things she looks for on the next page.

**Clean surroundings** – grass should be kept short and free from rubbish: no hiding place for snakes, rats or harmful insects.

**Latrine** – this should be 20 metres away from the house – separated from cooking and eating areas. The pit should be covered, about 6 metres deep if possible: less smell and fewer flies. The area round the latrine should be kept clean at all times.

**Kitchen** – this should be kept clean with covered containers for any stored food.

**Refuse pit** – burn as much rubbish as possible. The rest should be buried in a pit at a suitable distance from the village.

**Bathroom** – a screened for daily washing. Make sure is water for washing hands.

**Water source** – check that this is properly protected; no animals or clothes washing that can pass germs into the water.

**Dishrack** – each household should use a dishrack for drying dishes off the ground, away from animals.

**Drying line** – for blankets or clothes, away from lice or fleas.

Flora says goodbye and returns to the health centre. On the way, she examines a small roadside kiosk and foodstall for cleanliness and good produce.

Back in her office at the end of the day, Flora records the results of today's data collection for her monthly report.

The health inspector needs this information. It gives a clear picture of the way the community is living – what has improved, and where more needs to be done.

❝❝ But if there is a problem, I always discuss it with the community, so that everyone understands *why* these simple rules are important. ❞❞

*These mothers are learning to make the rehydration drink during a health centre clinic.*

# Clean water

More than half of the world's diseases are caused by dirty water. One of the most serious of these is cholera. Flora keeps a very careful watch on the villages she visits, especially in the rainy season. Cholera spreads very quickly from person to person and can soon affect a whole village.

❝ Cholera doesn't happen very often – but it can be deadly. It is most common in the rainy season. If I find someone has signs of cholera, such as very bad diarrhoea and vomiting, I report this immediately. The patient must be kept apart from others. There is no injection for this disease, but the sufferer should drink plenty of clean water in a rehydration drink, and we can help with other medicine, too. ❞

## Did you know?

**Diarrhoea** is a sign of several different diseases (including cholera), usually caused by germs from dirty water. The sick person loses a lot of water from their body – they become **dehydrated**, and this water must be replaced (rehydration). In babies and young children it is especially important to do this quickly.

**Rehydration drink**
1 litre clean water (boiled) + 2 big spoonfuls sugar + ½ teaspoonful salt

- A child needs at least one litre a day, given often, and in small amounts.

- An adult needs about three litres a day.

- Ready-mixed rehydration salts (available in small packets at the health centre) can also be added to clean water to make this drink.

Flora uses her village visits to remind people about the importance of clean water.

She shows them a special chemical mix called chlorine that can be added to water from the well to make it safe for cooking and drinking.

*Flora prepares a bucketful of chlorine mix. This can be stored, covered, for up to two weeks. A small spoonful of the mix added to a bucket of well-water will purify that water for drinking.*

While she waits for the chlorinated water to settle in the bucket, Flora talks to the group about the coming rainy season. She knows that malaria-carrying mosquitoes will increase during and immediately after the rainy season, so it is important to be prepared. What are the best ways of protecting yourself, she asks.

❝We encourage people to make, buy and use bednets whenever possible, especially for pregnant women and young children. They are most at risk from malaria. I explain that there are medicines for pregnant women if they come to our clinic, and that if a young child has a fever, quick treatment with anti-malaria medicine can be life-saving.❞

# Planning a family

An important part of Flora's job is to advise men and women about planning their families.

More than half of Malawi's young women have had a baby before they are twenty. It may mean that they cannot complete their education. This can cause problems for them. They need to find ways of making sure they do not have children before they are ready. Older parents who feel they have enough children need to know how to make sure they do not have any more.

Teaching family planning is a difficult part of Flora's job. Not everybody agrees about it – perhaps because of their religious or traditional beliefs.

❝ It's much more difficult than explaining how water has to be clean – everyone agrees about that! But there are definite health dangers for unplanned families. If a mother's children are born very close to each other, or there are very many children, the mother doesn't have time to get her strength back between births. If she becomes weak, the children suffer. ❞

Flora often gives talks about the family planning, and she explains the different methods of birth control, or contraception.

❝ I talk to husbands as well as wives, because they should decide together how to plan their families. My job is to explain what the choices are. It is important that people decide for themselves what they want to do. Many people still believe in big families, so change only comes slowly. ❞

## AIDS

Sometimes when Flora visits a village there are only a few people present.

❝ They tell me that everyone has gone to a funeral – often it's because another person has died as a result of AIDS. ❞

Flora understands just what a big problem AIDS is in her country. It has replaced every other disease as the leading cause of death, and has left many young children in the care of grandparents or other family members.

One of the problems is that the disease can take up to ten years to show itself, and during all that time, the infected person can pass the illness on to others. Flora has a very good reason for explaining the use of condoms to people – they can save lives.

❝ I give talks to people about AIDS. I use a special flip chart with pictures to show them how it spreads, and how important it is to use condoms. We also give out condoms free to people for their own protection. A number of diseases can be passed from one person to another when they have unprotected sex, but AIDS is the most deadly. ❞

*AIDS education in the community: using charts, children's puppet shows and drama or storytelling.*

*This 'mobile midwife' is visiting a pregnant mother at her home which is far from a hospital.*

# Bringing health care to the people

Two or three times a month, Flora visits each of the distant villages in the Mpemba area for an 'outreach' clinic.

❝❝ We travel on minibuses if we have funds; otherwise we walk. ❞❞

Mwangata is about two and a half hours' walk away from the health centre and Flora, the medical assistant and four other health workers set off early.

❝❝ It's a busy day for us all. We do immunisations, health and hygiene talks. The medical assistant gives medicines to children suffering from minor illnesses. We have to identify the very sick people in the village, and make sure they visit the health centre. ❞❞

Flora listens patiently to people's worries.

❝❝ One other mother wanted her baby to have a measles vaccination right away, but the baby was too young. I explained to her that giving a vaccination too early could harm her baby, and it was better to wait until our next visit. Once she understood this, she was happy. ❞❞

# Thinking about work

Flora is very clear about why she likes her job.

❝ I like communicating with other people. Although I give out information, I also learn a lot from the people I visit and talk to. This job makes you think about the real problems people sometimes face. ❞

Flora also finds that because she is a woman and a mother, other women are more trusting of her.

❝ Sometimes women are nervous about coming to the health centre because they are not sure whether there will be a female medical person there. I can reassure them about this, and help them to prepare for a visit. ❞

And what are the problems?

❝ The biggest practical problem I have is lack of transport. Walking to and from the villages takes up a lot of the day – and it's also quite tiring, when added to the daily walk to work. Sometimes I can go home after a village visit, but of course if there is an emergency, I must hurry back to the health centre and tell the medical staff right away. ❞

Flora looks forward to a future when people all over Malawi will be better informed about health.

❝ I think we will always need health workers because they are a link between the people and the medical help the government can provide. I'm always keen to learn more about health care myself so I can pass this on. ❞

*Flora at home at the end of the day.*

# Activities

## Health quiz

**1** Which of these things do people need to live healthy lives?

- a car
- clean water
- enough good food
- a home in a city
- nice clothes

What other things would you add to the list?

**2** Look at the picture below. Find two examples of good hygiene. How many health risks can you find? How would you correct these?

(*See page 15 for ideas.*)

## Make a health poster

Use pictures to show the importance of these things for good health:

- food
- water
- vaccinations

## Something to talk about

**1** What do you think is the most interesting part of Flora's job? What difficulties does she have?

**2** Imagine you are a health worker. Mrs Phiri's four-year-old grandson has got diarrhoea. What would you suggest?

(*See page 16 for ideas.*)